**W9-BVU-358**

6 -1- 05

Cell Specialization and Reproduction

Understanding How Cells Divide and Differentiate

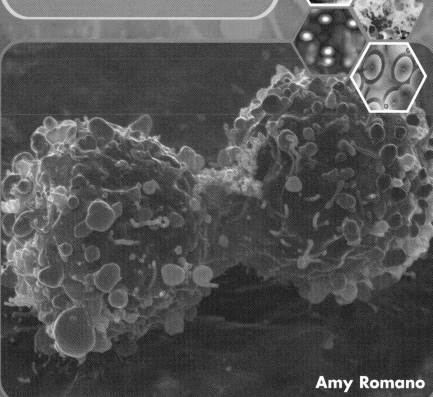

Amy Romano

The Rosen Publishing Group, Inc., New York

Published in 2005 by The Rosen Publishing Group, Inc.
29 East 21st Street, New York, NY 10010

Copyright © 2005 by The Rosen Publishing Group, Inc.

First Edition

Library of Congress Cataloging-in-Publication Data

Romano, Amy.
Cell specialization and reproduction: understanding how cells divide and differentiate/Amy Romano.—1st ed.
    p. cm.—(The library of cells)
Includes bibliographical references (p.   ).
ISBN 1-4042-0322-2 (library binding)
1. Cell differentiation—Juvenile literature. 2. Cell division—Juvenile literature.
I. Title. II. Series.
QH607.R66 2004
571.8'35—dc22
                                                    2004011252

Manufactured in the United States of America

On the cover: A color-enhanced scanning electron micrograph of a lung cancer cell during the process of cell division known as cytokinesis. Its two daughter cells remain temporarily joined by a cytoplasmic bridge *(center)*.

Contents

Introduction

Every living thing on the planet is made up of cells, small units sometimes called the building blocks of life. All cells are capable of consuming nutrients, expelling waste, and reproducing. Although some single cells are able to live independently (such as a bacterium or yeast), most have an extraordinary ability to join with other cells and communicate needs. These cellular groups work as a team to perform specific life functions. Most living creatures are multicellular organisms.

The larger the creature, the more cells it contains. Humans, for example, are made up of hundreds of millions (some say trillions) of individual cells. These cells combine to form tissues, tissues make up organs, and multiple organs form systems. Even the simplest cells in the human body are busy performing the processes necessary for life during every minute of every day. These functions include respiration, sensation, digestion, excretion, reproduction, and growth.

Before we can understand how cells grow and reproduce, however, we must first understand the components and functions of the cell itself.

Chapter One

Cell Types, Structures, and Functions

Cells vary in size, shape, function, and life span. Some cells will last your entire lifetime, while others may live for only a few days. All cells have a predetermined shape and size depending on their function. Skin cells, for example, are flat so they can pack tightly into layers. These layers of flat cells protect underlying tissues from bacteria, water, and the sun's damaging rays. Muscle cells, on the other hand, are longer and thinner. They are designed to be able to move your muscles through patterns of contracting and relaxing. Still different from these are nerve cells, or neurons. Nerve cells have a number of outstretched "arms" that help them send and receive chemical messages from other cells.

Skin, muscle, and nerve cells are all examples of specialized cells that are responsible for one specific job and exist as part of larger organisms. Other cells, such as amoebas, are self-sufficient, or capable of performing all necessary functions to sustain life on their own.

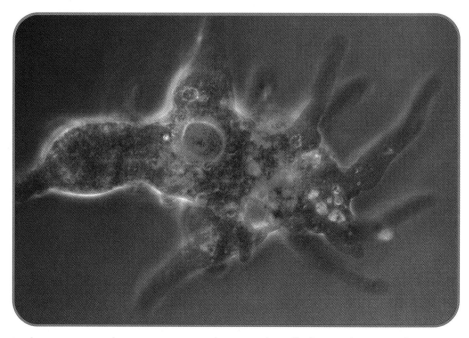

In this scanning electron micrograph, a single-celled amoeba extends its pseudopods, or "false feet." Its large circular nucleus and vacuoles appear pink inside blue-colored cytoplasm. In order to move, the amoeba extends its pseudopod in the direction it wants to go, anchors it, and pulls itself forward by contracting its body. Pseudopodia are also used to engulf food that is digested within the amoeba's internal vacuoles.

Prokaryotic and Eukaryotic Cells

There are two main types of cell classifications. The simplest cells are known as prokaryotic cells. Prokaryotic cells are found largely in organisms classified as bacteria. A prokaryote is a cell that does not have a true nucleus. The components of the prokaryote, including the chromosomes that carry its DNA (deoxyribonucleic acid), mingle freely in its interior compartment, called a nucleoid.

Prokaryotes are simple cells that are wrapped in a flexible, saclike covering called a plasma membrane,

This illustration of a prokaryotic bacterium cell identifies its main parts. An external cell wall and a plasma membrane surround it. A single flagellum gives the cell mobility. Inside, its ribosomes are contained in a jellylike cytoplasm. Prokaryotic cells do not have a true nucleus.

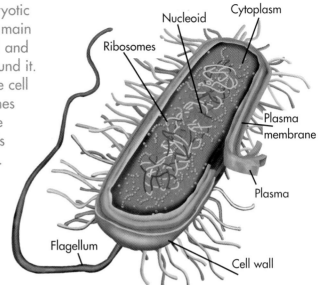

Nucleoid

Cytoplasm

Ribosomes

Plasma membrane

Plasma

Flagellum

Cell wall

which is surrounded by a cell wall. The plasma membrane contains tiny pores, or openings, that allow molecules to pass into and out of the cell. There is little diversity among prokaryotic cells. They are generally rodlike, spiral, or round in shape.

Prokaryotic cells, although simple, perform a variety of processes and activities. In fact, prokaryotic cells have a much broader range of biochemical reactions than their relatives, eukaryotic cells, do.

Eukaryotic cells do not appear more complex than prokaryotic cells do, but they are more organized and efficient. Unlike the prokaryotic cells of bacteria, all the components of eukaryotic cells are housed in a number of interior compartments called organelles, or "little organs." The largest organelle in a eukaryotic cell is the nucleus. The nucleus is the cell's control center. It contains the chromosomes, which carry the cell's DNA.

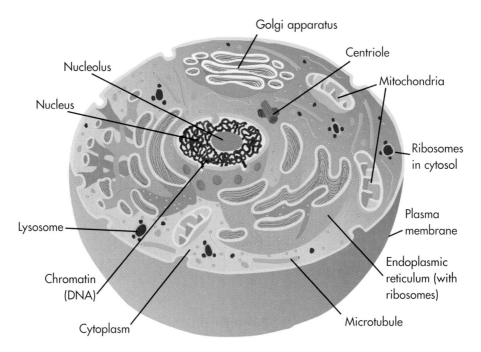

Golgi apparatus

Centriole

Nucleolus

Mitochondria

Nucleus

Ribosomes
in cytosol

Plasma
membrane

Lysosome

Endoplasmic
reticulum (with
ribosomes)

Chromatin
(DNA)

Microtubule

Cytoplasm

Eukaryotic cells are easily identifiable by their nuclei. This illustration identifies all the internal organelles of an animal cell inside the jellylike cytoplasm including its vacuoles, mitochondria, endoplasmic reticulum, Golgi apparatus, lysosomes, ribosomes, and centrioles. The cell's nucleus is located at the center, surrounded by chromatin-containing DNA. Eukaryotic cells are protected by a semipermeable plasma membrane.

Regardless of a cell's size, shape, function, or type, and regardless of whether it is self-sufficient or part of a larger organism, all eukaryotic cells have a number of structural components that serve specific purposes.

What's Inside?

The common parts of prokaryotic and eukaryotic cells include the plasma membrane mentioned earlier; a jellylike interior known as cytoplasm, which excludes the nucleus; and tiny, beadlike structures called ribosomes and chromosomes.

The plasma membrane is a semipermeable wall that allows specific material to exit and enter the cell. If cells didn't have these semipermeable walls, they would have no way to obtain nourishment or excrete waste. The cytoplasm of eukaryotic cells contains organelles, which each serve a different function. The cytoplasm of both eukaryotic and prokaryotic cells also contains complex compounds, chemicals, and DNA, the hereditary material that is present in all cells. DNA contains the genetically coded instructions for all cell functions, including growth and reproduction.

Cell Organelles

As previously mentioned, the largest organelle, the nucleus, is found only in eukaryotic cells. The nucleus is the cell's "brain"; it controls most of the cell's activities. The nucleus is connected to other organelles through a network of canals in the cytoplasm. These canals are called the endoplasmic reticulum.

The endoplasmic reticulum takes two forms: rough and smooth. It serves as the cell's circulatory system and keeps cytoplasm, proteins, and other molecules flowing through the cell in an orderly fashion.

The proteins within the cell are largely produced by a number of tiny particles called ribosomes. Messages are sent from the cell's nucleus to the ribosomes via a substance known as ribonucleic acid (RNA). RNA is chemically similar to DNA, but it consists of a different single strand of sugar. Two types of RNA, messenger RNA (mRNA) and transfer RNA (tRNA), work together to tell the ribosomes which amino acids need to be combined to form the proteins necessary for cell growth.

As the protein factory within the cell, ribosomes also work closely with the Golgi apparatus, which stores excess proteins. The protein is then transported wherever and whenever it is needed. It acts as a catalyst (substance that provokes change) for various cell functions, such as growth.

Other important organelles are the oval-shaped mitochondria, known as the powerhouse of the cell. The mitochondria are where glucose (sugar) and other nutrients are converted into adenosine triphosphate (ATP). ATP is a molecule that serves as the energy source for cellular processes such as respiration and waste removal.

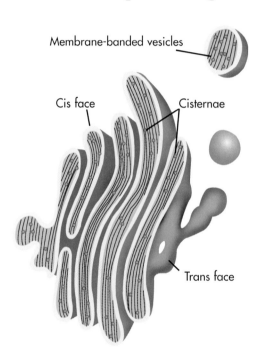

Membrane-banded vesicles

Cis face

Cisternae

Trans face

This image shows a eukaryotic cell's Golgi apparatus and its many flattened membrane-bounded sacs that look like deflated balloons. The function of this organelle is to sort the cell's proteins and lipids (fats). The apparatus's cis face ("cis" means "on the near side of") is identified, as well as its trans face ("trans" means "beyond it").

Mysterious Mitochondria

Mitochondria are among the most interesting organelles. They are the only organelles able to work independently from the cell nucleus. Because mitochondria have similar characteristics to those of the self- sustaining prokaryotes (no nucleus, similar DNA and ribosomal structure, independent cell division through binary fission [reproduction]), scientists have developed a theory about mitochondrial origins.

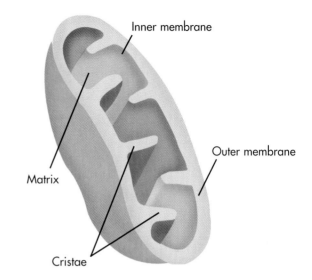

Inner membrane

Outer membrane

Matrix

Cristae

Mitochondria are oblong-shaped organelles with an inner and outer membrane. Depending on its size, the cell might have several mitochondria, which act as its "power generators." The mitochondria convert oxygen and nutrients into energy, or ATP.

This theory, called the endosymbiosis hypothesis, claims that millions of years ago, mitochondria were free-living prokaryotes capable of aerobic respiration and reproduction. Aerobic respiration is a process in which oxygen must be present to convert nutrients into energy. At some point, these prokaryotes were engulfed by other, larger eukaryotes, but were not digested. Scientists believe this resulted in two cells that developed a symbiotic, or cooperative, relationship.

The cohabitation of these two independent cells required the host eukaryotic cell to provide essential nutrients. At the same time, the engulfed prokaryotic cell used these nutrients to carry out aerobic respiration and provide the host cell with ATP. Ultimately, it is believed that the engulfed cells evolved into mitochondria, essential organelles that retain the DNA and ribosomal characteristics of their prokaryotic ancestors.

Cell Functions

In order to live, cells must carry out a number of different functions. Although not all cells can do all things, most must be able to move, ingest food and convert it to energy, recycle molecules and expel waste, and reproduce. These basic functions enable cells to respond to changes in their environment, adapt accordingly, and continue to live.

Motion

Single-celled prokaryotic organisms are able to move in a gliding motion with the help of a flagellum, a long tail-like structure made of protein. Movement is essential for all single-celled organisms to aid them in getting food, oxygen, and other substances necessary for life. Most eukaryotic cells, on the other hand, achieve movement with the help of structures called cilia. Cilia are short, hairlike proteins that extend from and cover the surface of the cell. Cells move the cilia to propel them where they need to go.

Other eukaryotic cells move in a crawling motion that is referred to as amoeboid movement. To perform amoeboid movement, cytoplasm presses against the

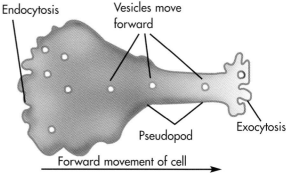

Endocytosis

Vesicles move forward

Pseudopod

Exocytosis

Forward movement of cell

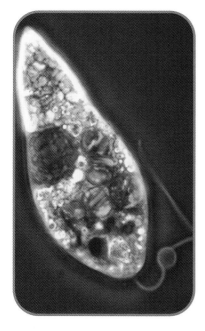

The motion of freshwater euglena *(left)*, a single-celled protozoan, by its long, taillike flagellum, can be seen in this electron micrograph. The process by which an amoeba contracts its cytoplasm inward to create a pseudopod *(right)* is called endocytosis. The reverse outward projection of its cytoplasmic pseudopod is called exocytosis.

cell membrane and creates a temporary "foot" that extends from the cell. This false foot drags the trailing end of the cell to a new position. The process is repeated until the cell is where it wants to be.

Lysosomes

Smaller and rounder than mitochondria, but no less important, lysosomes are small organelles that function as the cell's "recycling center." Containing powerful enzymes that aid in digestion, lysosomes break down worn-out organelles, unused proteins, lipids (fats), and other molecules the cell recognizes as waste.

Nutrition and Energy

Regardless of type, all cells require food for energy. They consume a variety of foods, ranging from simple nutrients dissolved in water that enter into the cell via the plasma membrane, to other smaller organisms. Amoebas, for example, are capable of engulfing and absorbing their food.

Mitochondria are the organelles responsible for maintaining the balance between food and energy. Before cells can convert any nutrient to energy, the cell must extract the nutrient and convert it to ATP.

Respiration

In a typical cell, thousands of ATP molecules are created each second. Most eukaryotic cells use oxygen to convert glucose (sugar) into ATP through a process known as aerobic (meaning "with oxygen") respiration. Aerobic respiration occurs constantly within a cell. If it ceases, the cell—and ultimately the organism—dies.

ATP molecules can also be created without oxygen through a process called anaerobic (meaning "without oxygen") respiration, also known as fermentation. Fermentation is the process by which single-celled eukaryotes, like yeast, build ATP.

Chapter Two

Cell Reproduction

New cells must be made in order for living things to grow. These new cells are created through a process known as reproduction. Reproduction is how all living things produce offspring. Reproduction is also how an organism ensures its survival even while other organisms around it grow old, get damaged, or die.

All cells reproduce via cell division. Based on the name, you might think that the cell simply divides the DNA it already has to create a new cell. Simply dividing the DNA present in a single cell between two new cells, however, would lead to disaster. The two new cells would have different and incomplete genetic instructions. Future generations of these cells would have even less information. In order to function properly, each new cell needs a *complete* copy of the parent cell's genetic information.

Whether the purpose is to grow bigger or to repair or replace damaged or dying cells, biologists estimate that approximately 25 million cells in the human body go through some form of cell division every second!

DNA

"DNA" is an abbreviation for "deoxyribonucleic acid." It is an organic chemical found in all prokaryotic and eukaryotic cells. DNA carries the genetic information that controls all inherited traits.

DNA was first discovered in 1869; however, its role in genetics was not determined until years later. In 1953, biophysicists James Watson and Francis Crick discovered that DNA is a double-helix (spiral-shaped) polymer consisting of two intertwined strands.

The DNA molecule is stable, allowing it to act as a template for the replication of new DNA molecules, as well as for the replication of the related RNA molecules.

In this representation of a segment of the molecule deoxyribonucleic acid (DNA), color-coded spheres depict various atoms in the molecule. DNA is composed of two strands, which are twisted together. In this image, its outer sugar phosphate atoms are colored blue, while its inner base atoms are colored light blue.

Mitosis

The simplest method of cell reproduction involves only one parent cell. In this method, the parent cell divides into two or more similar parts, each of which becomes a new cell. This type of reproduction is known as asexual reproduction. It occurs via a process called mitosis (also known as eukaryotic reproduction). Nearly all cells in the human body reproduce asexually.

In mitosis, the nucleus divides in half to form two new "daughter" cells, each with a full set of chromosomes. This type of division is essential for life to continue. Without it, cells would likely die after only a few days.

There are five recognized stages of mitosis: prophase, metaphase, anaphase, telophase, and cytokinesis. Before these stages begin, however, the cell goes through an indistinguishable period called interphase. During interphase, the cell makes an exact and complete copy of the DNA of each chromosome. A chromosome is a long, threadlike structure composed of DNA and proteins that contains a cell's genetic information. Once the DNA copy is complete, the cell prepares to divide by going through the remaining distinct phases.

Prophase

Now that the DNA copy is complete, each chromosome is composed of two paired structures called chromatids. Chromatids are the two chromosome strands that develop during cell division. In prophase, these chromatids get shorter and thicker until they appear to join at a single site. This site, known as the centromere, is the point at which two parts of a chromosome join and to which the spindle fibers are attached during mitosis. The spindle fibers pull the chromatids toward the middle of the cell. Because the DNA of the parent cell has already been copied, these chromatids are exact copies of each other. Before the cell can divide, however, the chromatids must separate.

As the nuclear membrane starts to break down and the pairs start to break apart, thin fibers appear and a structure known as the spindle is created.

Metaphase

In metaphase, the still-attached chromatids line up along their centromeres at the middle of the cell.

Anaphase

Next, in anaphase, the chromatid pairs split apart at the centromeres and each half of the pair moves to opposite sides (poles) of the cells.

Telophase

Telophase is like the prophase in reverse. The chromosomes have reached the opposite poles of the cell, the spindle disappears, the nuclear membrane forms again, and the chromosomes expand into thin strands of chromatin. Chromatin is the foundation for forming chromosomes, and contains DNA, RNA, and various proteins.

Cytokinesis

Mitosis ends with the formation of two new cells, each with a matching and complete set of chromosomes, as well as an identical composition of cellular structures. Once the division of the nucleus is com-

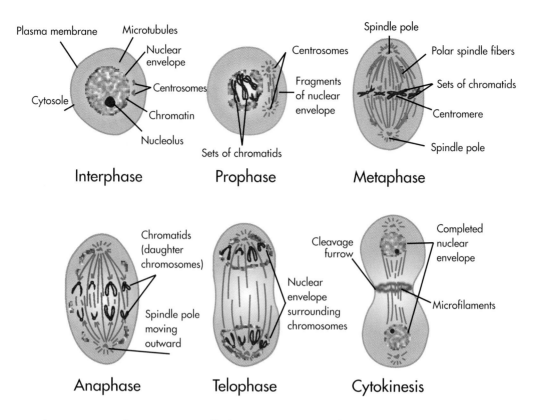

Interphase — Plasma membrane, Microtubules, Nuclear envelope, Centrosomes, Chromatin, Nucleolus, Cytosole

Prophase — Centrosomes, Fragments of nuclear envelope, Sets of chromatids

Metaphase — Spindle pole, Polar spindle fibers, Sets of chromatids, Centromere, Spindle pole

Anaphase — Chromatids (daughter chromosomes), Spindle pole moving outward

Telophase — Cleavage furrow, Nuclear envelope surrounding chromosomes

Cytokinesis — Completed nuclear envelope, Microfilaments

The process of mitosis, or cell division occurs in five steps, beginning after interphase *(top left)* a preliminary period in which the cell increases in size and its DNA is replicated. The final step of mitosis is cytokinesis *(bottom right)* the actual division of the cell into two daughter cells, each with its own nucleus.

plete, the cytoplasm divides. The cell membrane contracts and pinches the cell between the two nuclei until the cytoplasm separates into two new daughter cells. Mitosis is also how the body grows and replaces cells throughout its life span.

Although it is a simple, reliable way of dividing and multiplying, mitosis has one very important disadvantage: the lack of genetic variability. This means that the cell and its resulting organisms never obtain any new characteristics (traits). It may require a longer period to adapt to environmental changes or to fight disease. This inability to adapt in the face of change is the reason that most animals, including humans, reproduce sexually, not asexually.

Meiosis

Unlike mitosis, meiosis, or sexual reproduction, ensures genetic variability. It uses a second type of cell division. In humans, female eggs, produced in the ovaries, and male sperm, produced in the testes, are gametes. Unlike the process that occurs in mitosis, meiosis does not create clones of the parent cell. It uses sex cells that will join with other sex cells to produce offspring.

During meiosis, two cell divisions occur. The result is four new daughter cells. These are called haploid cells, each with a single set of chromosomes, only half the total number of chromosomes as the parent cell. These two divisions are known as meiosis I and meiosis II.

Meiosis I

In the first cell division of meiosis, the chromosomes of a diploid cell (a cell with a double set of chromosomes) duplicate and join in pairs. Each pair has duplicate chromatids (identical copies of chromosomes). The paired chromosomes (each known as a tetrad) align at the center of the cell and then separate and move to opposite poles in the cell. As with mitosis, the cell then splits to form two daughter cells identical to the parent cell.

Meiosis II

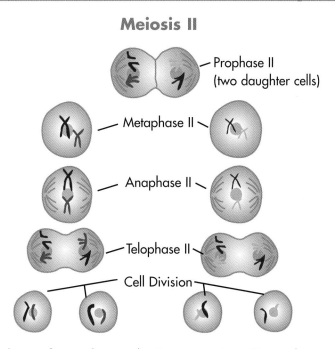

Prophase II
(two daughter cells)

Metaphase II

Anaphase II

Telophase II

Cell Division

The second phase of sexual reproduction, or meiosis II, can be seen in these illustrations. In the preceding meiotic division, or meiosis I (not illustrated), the chromosomes in the diploid cell contracted and maternal and paternal chromosomes joined at the middle of the cell. At that stage, each pair of chromosomes is called a tetrad. Each tetrad is pulled to opposite ends of the cell (telophase I) to form two new "daughter" cells. In meiosis II, the steps of which are shown in this diagram, each daughter cell divides once, and then again.

Meiosis II

As meiosis proceeds, the two daughter cells undergo another cell division to form a total of four cells, each of which bears half the number of chromosomes found in the other cells of the organism. The resulting sex cells include instructions called genes, which are located on the chromosomes. Genes carry codes that determine the characteristics that will be inherited.

Meiosis ensures that reproduction results in a zygote with a full set of chromosomes: one-half of a set from the male parent and one-half of a set from the female parent. By definition, a zygote is a fertilized ovum in the pre-embryonic stage. When two gametes unite to form a zygote, the full number of chromosomes, known as the diploid number, is restored and growth can begin. Some organisms that sexually reproduce are fungi and animals, including humans.

One Cell, One Job

As an organism grows, only certain cells continue to divide. Although both skin and blood cells continually replenish in humans, nerve cells and muscle cells do not. Nerve and muscle cells don't divide or continue to grow after early childhood. This permits cells of multicellular organisms to specialize and focus on their most-needed functions.

All multicellular organisms begin life as single cells. They multiply using the process of mitosis and develop into complex organisms that contain billions of cells, and then undergo meiosis to sexually reproduce. In full-grown organisms, mitosis continues as a means of replacing dying or damaged cells.

Regardless of the type of cell or which reproduction process it undergoes, ongoing development occurs in three stages: growth, movement, and differentiation.

Chapter Three

Natural Differentiation

The human body consists of more than 200 different types of cells. Those that look alike and work together to perform the same function are called tissues. Tissues work together to form organs, and organs work together to form systems. Since all cells begin with the same composition and similar goals and functions, how do specialized cells become specialized? How do they know what job they are meant for?

In the beginning, all cells have the same set of chromosomes that contains the instructions for the entire organism. As cells divide, however, certain genes within the cell's DNA are activated, while others remain dormant. Because genes control the production of protein, and different proteins result in different cellular characteristics, cells become more specialized with each division. This process of specialization is called differentiation.

Scientists are still learning how differentiation works and are still in the process of discovering the catalyst that turns certain genes "on" or "off." A catalyst is something that initiates or makes things change. Scientists hope to someday be able to use these "on-off switches" to help repair damaged organs, or even grow new body parts in a process called controlled differentiation. Today, however, the human body's naturally differentiated cells are represented, in part, by the following cell types.

Nerve and Messenger Cells

From the day you are born, your body has all the neurons (nerve cells) it will ever contain. Neurons never increase in quantity and have a very limited capability to repair themselves if damaged. Don't worry, though; we are born with billions and billions of neurons that reside in the brain, spinal cord, and other areas throughout the body. Neurons are responsible for communicating needs and controlling the information shared between

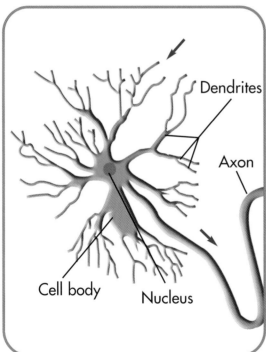

This is a diagram of a typical neuron, or nerve cell. The red arrows indicate the direction in which signals are transported. The single axon (center) conducts signals away from the cell, while dendrites process signals from the axons to other neurons.

Dendrites

Axon

Cell body

Nucleus

cells. In fact, the human body contains more than 10 billion individual neurons, each with a nucleus.

Approximately 100 microscopic fibers called dendrites reach out from each neuron. Dendrites transmit signals, or impulses, from outside the cell body. While the dendrites communicate information from outside the cell inward, small fibers called axons control the communications carried away from the neuron. These communications between neurons occur as an electrical impulse passed over a microscopic gap called a synapse.

The body's neurons form a complex communication network called the nervous system. The nervous system is a complex electrical system that controls every voluntary and involuntary action we make, including sensing what we see, hear, taste, smell, and feel, as well as how we think or respond to various situations, or stimuli.

Bone and Skin Cells

Most of the 206 bones in your body were formed by the time you were born. Bones form the body's skeleton, its framework, and help protect its delicate nerves and muscles. Both bone and skin cells are considered living tissue. Both continually produce new cells and are able to heal themselves when damaged.

Specialized cells called osteocytes produce new bone cells. Osteocytes secrete a protein into which minerals are deposited. These minerals, primarily calcium carbonate and calcium phosphate, account for the majority of a bone's weight.

While bones are a body's frame, skin can be seen as a body's wrapper. Skin is the body's largest organ. It grows faster than any other organ does, and it has the ability to continually replace lost and damaged cells over time. The skin is made up of two layers, the epidermis and the dermis. The epidermis, the skin's outer layer, is a tough, waterproof, protective layer. It is composed of dead cells that contain a protein called keratin. The dermis, or inner layer, is thicker than the epidermis and gives the skin its strength and elasticity.

Blood Cells

Blood cells are another example of specialized cells. Essentially a moving "tissue," blood carries oxygen and nutrients to the potentially trillions of cells that make up the entire human body. Once the delivery is complete, the blood is responsible for removing waste, such as carbon dioxide.

Blood is made up of red and white blood cells, hemoglobin, and platelets, all existing within a yellowish, watery substance called plasma. Red blood cells transport oxygen to the body's cells. Hemoglobin, a substance made of protein and iron, is responsible for blood's red coloration. Red blood cells are continually produced in the interior marrow of the long bones in the human body. The life span of an individual red blood cell is only about four months.

White blood cells are two to three times larger than red blood cells. Called leukocytes, there are only about two white blood cells for every 1,000 red blood cells. Despite this imbalance, white blood cells are charged with the difficult task of "eating" bacteria and other invaders that may attack healthy red blood cells.

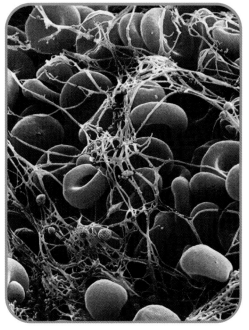

An arterial thrombus, or a blood clot that remains in its place of origin in the body, is pictured in this electron micrograph. This image shows erythrocytes, the red blood cells that carry oxygen to all other body cells, as well as platelets (colored with a blue dye), and fibrin (yellow threads), the "clotting factor" that forms to bind the cells together.

The final components in blood, platelets, are also continually produced in bone marrow. Although their life span is also short, the job of platelets is very important. Platelets release a substance that helps blood clot, thus stopping your body from bleeding when you cut yourself.

Muscle Cells

Muscle cells are responsible for your body's movement. There are three kinds of muscle cells in your body: striated (voluntary) cells; smooth (involuntary)

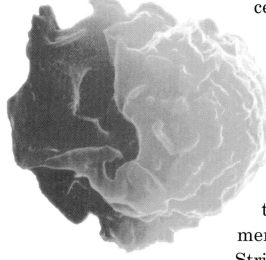

cells; and heart cells. All muscle cells share the ability to contract (shorten) and relax (lengthen). There are more than 650 muscles in your body that work together to make movement possible.

Lymphocytes, like the one shown here, are white blood cells important to both humans and animals to ward off disease. Lymphocytes respond to foreign molecules in the body. B lymphocytes (B cells) produce antibody molecules; T lymphocytes (T cells) recognize and respond to foreign molecules.

Striated muscles allow for quick actions such as walking or turning your head. These muscles are strengthened through exercise. Although striated muscles may get bigger and stronger, the actual number of muscle cells a person has remains constant throughout his or her life.

Involuntary muscles are more sluggish than their striated counterparts. As such, we have little or no control over their actions. The actions of involuntary muscles are largely directed by changes in the body's chemistry or by signals from surrounding nerve cells.

The heart muscle is the hardest-working muscle in the human body. It is classified as involuntary, but it has a number of physical characteristics of the striated muscle group. The human heart beats

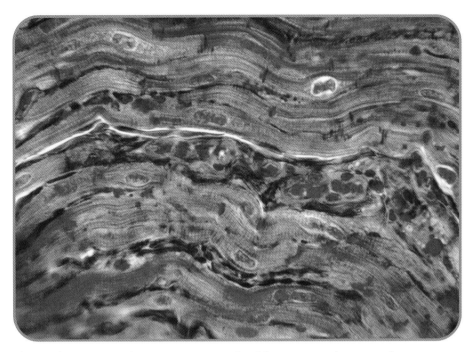

Shown here is an electron micrograph of human cardiac muscle tissue. The cardiac muscle produces the heartbeat. Adjacent muscle cells in the heart are electrically linked, which causes the cells to collectively help the muscle tissue contract in synchronicity.

sixty to eighty times each minute, every minute of every day of your life. It pumps about 1,250 gallons (4,732 liters) of blood throughout your body every single day.

Benefits of Differentiation

As we have discussed, cells are different in chemical composition, structure, and purpose as they develop and grow. This differentiation is essential. It has also been cited as scientific validation for the theory of evolution. Differentiation is largely possible because of special cells known as stem cells.

Although not yet entirely understood, research has shown that stem cells are the foundation of all the specialized cells of a mature organism.

Scientists have learned that if they can isolate and study cells as they develop, and then control certain stages of cell development, they might some-day find the key that unlocks the mysteries of the world's deadliest diseases.

Chapter Four

Specialization by Design

Since first observed under a microscope in 1665, by Englishman Robert Hooke, scientists have been trying to understand cell processes. Until recently, however, researchers have not been able to isolate and study the functions of individual cells or determine their impact on the larger organisms they support. As advancements in research technologies and techniques continue, we have more and more access to virtually every organelle, every enzyme, and every protein in a single cell.

In 1995, for example, the Nobel Prize was awarded to three biologists for their discovery of individual genes that control the position of different body parts in fruit flies. They discovered that if even one of these genes is defective, the wrong kind of body part may develop or the same body part may be duplicated in several different places. It was their hope that by isolating and studying these genes, they could someday help children born with limb deformities or victims of amputation.

This is an extreme example of what could be done if scientists fully understood and could control cell development. However, it is the study of how individual cells specialize that will result in new and better ways of diagnosing, treating, and even preventing a variety of illnesses.

Despite the potential that a greater understanding of cell differentiation holds, the controversy surrounding genetic engineering (the manipulation of human cells) has stopped a number of research initiatives. At the center of the controversy is the process of cloning (the artificial production of an organism genetically identical to its parent) and stem cell research (the study and manipulation of undifferentiated embryonic cells).

Cloning

The controlled or guided process of cloning has sparked a fiery battle in a number of political, religious, and medical forums. The asexual reproductive process of mitosis is, essentially, cloning. In mitosis, an exact copy of the parent organism (or clone) is created.

In the laboratory, cloning began when scientists began controlling the process of mitosis. Later, they used animal embryos in their experiments. During these more complex trials, the scientists were able to control the cellular development of an organism from a fertilized egg to an exact, full-grown copy of the original organism.

Then, in the 1950s, scientists experimented with undifferentiated embryonic cells.

Scientists working for PPL Therapeutics in London, England, in 2002 cloned these five piglets. The company made claims that organs from the animals were the first of their kind that could be used for human organ transplants. PPL Therapeutics also created Dolly, the cloned sheep.

Undifferentiated cells (stem cells) have not yet specialized into a particular type of cell. Scientists also confirmed these cells to be totipotent (able to give rise to all the different cell types in the body). To explore this cellular flexibility, scientists developed three techniques to clone embryonic cells: blastomere separation, blastocyst division, and somatic cell nuclear transfer.

Blastomere Separation

In blastomere separation, an egg cell is fertilized with a sperm cell in a laboratory dish. The embryo is allowed to divide until it forms a body of about four cells. Scientists then remove the exterior coating of the embryo and immerse it in a liquid. This solution encourages the individual cells of the embryo, known as blastomeres, to separate. Each blastomere is then put in a culture where it forms another embryo containing the same genetic composition as the original. Each new embryo can then be implanted into the uterus of a surrogate mother with the ability to develop as any other embryo would during a normal pregnancy.

Blastocyst Division

Blastocyst division differs slightly from blastomere separation in that scientists allow a fertilized egg to divide until it forms a mass of about 32 to 150 cells, known as a blastocyst. The researchers then split the blastocyst in two parts and implant both halves into the uterus of a surrogate mother. The two halves then develop as identical twins.

Somatic Cell Nuclear Transfer

With both blastomere separation and blastocyst division, the clone contains the genetic material from both a mother and father. In contrast, cloning via somatic cell nuclear transfer produces an embryo carrying the genetic material of only one parent. Scientists transfer the genetic material from a donor's somatic cell, any body cell other than a sex cell, to an egg cell that has had its own nucleus, and therefore its DNA, removed. The resulting cloned cell contains the genetic material of the donor's somatic cell only.

Early somatic cell transfer experiments worked only when using cells from embryonic or immature animals. In 1997, however, British scientists successfully cloned a sheep named Dolly using adult somatic cells. With Dolly's birth, a new scientific path was discovered. Although undifferentiated embryonic cells were easier to work with, they could be unpredictable. After the Dolly experiment, scientists were better able to predict the physical characteristics of the clone because they were starting with an adult.

Although Dolly was not warmly received by much of the world, her existence, and the fact that she was later able to become pregnant and deliver her own offspring, is a testament to the medical promises inherent in cloning. Through cloning, scientists can develop a greater understanding of genetics and development and how to manipulate organisms. They can study how cells adapt as the needs of the parent organism change. And they can identify the roles both genes and the environment play in determining an individual's health.

Stem Cell Research

Stem cells used in cytology (the study of cells) and cloning have shown that they may also provide

Donor nucleus

Egg cell

Fused cell

Embryo

In February 1997, British scientists successfully cloned a sheep named Dolly. This illustration shows how Dolly was formed from a single zygote, or fertilized egg. The process by which Dolly was created is called somatic cell nuclear transfer. Before Dolly was cloned, scientists were unsure if one single donor cell could actually be genetically totipotent, or able to develop all of the specialized cells needed for life and natural (sexual) reproduction.

powerful information for additional biological research. In addition to being a catalyst for cloning, it is believed that stem cells could serve as starting points in the treatment of a wide variety of diseases including Alzheimer's, Parkinson's, diabetes, and multiple sclerosis.

Some researchers believe that with enough time and attention, stem cell research could not only result in the ability to identify genetic indicators (markers) for various diseases, but also provide more effective treatments for them. Stem cells may even provide future cures for illnesses that today we can only manage. Some people, however, maintain that just because stem cells can provide this information, it doesn't mean we should utilize it.

The controversy surrounding stem cell research is intense. Although scientists have been using stem cells in their research since the 1950s, religious, political, moral, and medical arguments are made in favor of and against stem cell research on a daily basis. The first successful bone marrow transplant, a procedure that was first performed in 1968, infused healthy bone marrow cells into diseased bone marrow in order to restore blood-making capabilities, is a perfect example of the positive medical advancement that the research of stem cells helped provide. Researchers have long believed that the stem cells within the bone marrow are the cells that made this technique successful.

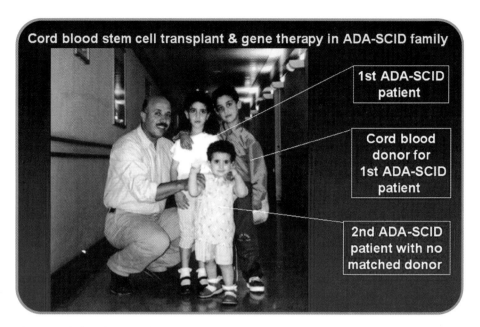

Cord blood stem cell transplant & gene therapy in ADA-SCID family

1st ADA-SCID patient

Cord blood donor for 1st ADA-SCID patient

2nd ADA-SCID patient with no matched donor

The Israeli family seen here, two-year old Salsabil Abu Sa'ad (foreground), her father, Taher (left), sister, Tasmin (center), and brother, Adbel (right), benefited from stem cell research and treatment when Salsabil was completely cured from severe combined immunodeficiency, or ADA-SCID. Israeli professor Shimon Slavin was able to help doctors cure the youngster in 2002, by using genetically altered stem cells after she was born without an immune system. She became the world's first child to be completely cured of the disease by using stem cells.

Bone marrow transplants are now a standard therapy for certain cancers, such as leukemia and lymphoma, as well as for other diseases of the blood and bones.

As the twentieth century ended, however, researchers had not yet developed any medical treatments that relied solely on isolated stem cells grown in a culture. There is overwhelming recent scientific evidence that isolating stem cells as a process of genetic engineering is indeed a path that could lead to medical miracles.

Chapter Five

The Future

The issues of cloning and stem cell research have been hotly debated for the past several decades. Critics argue that the science of cloning is too young. The fears are twofold: in order to achieve success, researchers first must fail. This failure would result in cloned animals or humans with serious defects. The second fear is that without proper regulation, cloning opens the door for genetically designed babies.

Fundamental objections to stem cell research are founded in the questions: Where do stem cells come from? Should stem cells be considered human or human tissue? Some stem cells come from human embryos, so for opponents who believe that life begins at conception, stem cell research involves the destruction of a human life and should be forever prohibited. Supporters of stem cell research claim that because an embryo cannot exist independently, it cannot develop into a full human being. In other words, they believe that embryos that will not reach full development—such as those cloned from donated human eggs—should be used for ongoing stem cell research.

Elizabeth Blackburn (above), made far-reaching discoveries in 1984 about how humans might be predisposed to cancerous cell growth. In 2004, Blackburn made headlines because she was fired from the President's Council of Bioethics. While Blackburn insists she was let go because she is an advocate for stem cell research, White House officials say she was fired because the council was "moving away from its discussion of . . . stem cell research."

Despite the international controversy, President George W. Bush announced in 2001 that federal funding would be made available for stem cell research, but only for research on existing stem cells. This means that already existing stem cell cultures could be used in federally funded projects, but scientists were not allowed to isolate future stem cells. Researchers who did not agree to adhere to these guidelines were not eligible for federal funding.

The science of cloning is in its infancy. Critics argue that in order for scientists to achieve success, mistakes will most likely be made along the way. These mistakes, it is feared, could result in the development of cloned animals or humans with serious defects. Other critics fear that the cloning process tampers with the will of nature. Because of this controversy, the future of cloning remains uncertain.

Medical procedures, such as the transplanting of fetal stem cells into adults, remain experimental. Someday, however, researchers hope to use cloning to artificially create animals with a variety of human diseases. They could then use these cloned animals to test the safety and effectiveness of new treatments. This process, if it's ever acted upon, could potentially improve the quality of life for hundreds of thousands of human beings around the world.

In 2001, the first clinical trial testing the transplant of fetal stem cells was conducted. Researchers injected stem cells into the brains of patients suffering from Parkinson's disease. The results were mixed. Although the injected cells did grow, the treatment produced no obvious benefits for patients age sixty and older, the group most often afflicted with Parkinson's. Some of the patients under age sixty, however, said they did feel better after the treatment. According to a 2003 report in the science journal *Nature*, 2001 and 2003 stem cell transplants for Parkinson's patients were failures. In the 2003 experiment, 50 percent of the patients suffered "jerky, involuntary movements," or dyskinesisas, as a side effect.

In 2004, the ethics of cloning and stem cell research once again rose to the international stage

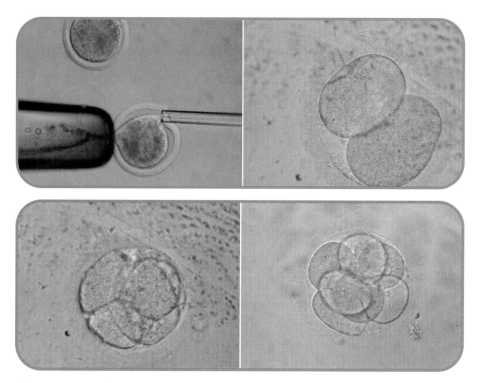

These images show the process used by South Korean doctors who successfully cloned a human embryo for the first time. The pictures *(clockwise from top left),* show the injection of a donor cell; the cloned embryo at the two-cell stage; four-cell stage; and eight-cell stage. The cloning experiment, which was conducted in South Korea, was reported in the journal *Science.* It was not done to create human babies, but to form stem cells that could grow into any tissue.

following a successful cloning of human embryos by South Korean scientists. The scientists extracted a line of stem cells from a cloned embryo. In the process, the embryos were destroyed. Although this research could not have been legally carried out in the United States, the proof that we do, in fact, have the ability to extract embryonic stem cells from cloned embryos was regarded as a breakthrough achievement in science.

Glossary

asexual reproduction (AY-seks-yoo-ul ree-pro-DUK-shun) The division of a parent cell into two or more similar pieces, each of which becomes a new cell.

biology (by-AH-luh-jee) The study of living organisms.

cell (SEL) The basic unit of life.

cell membrane (SEL MEM-brayn) Semipermeable outer layer of the cell body.

cell theory (SEL THEER-ee) Belief that all living things are made up of cells.

centromere (SEN-troh-meer) The point at which two parts of a chromosome join.

chromosome (KRO-moh-sohm) Threadlike structure in a cell's nucleus that carries DNA.

cloning (KLO-ning) A process that produces a cell, cell product, or organism that contains genetic material identical to the original.

cytoplasm (SY-toh-plaz-um) The jellylike interior of a cell.

differentiation (DIH-fuh-rent-shee-ay-shun) A process by which cells become different and specialized.

deoxyribonucleic acid (DEE-ox-ee-ry-boh-noo-klay-ik AH-sid) Also called DNA. The molecules of genes; the chemical basis of hereditary traits.

eukaryote (yoo-KAYR-ee-oht) A cell that contains a nucleus surrounded by a membrane.

fertilization (fer-til-ih-ZAY-shun) The joining together of a male and female sex cell to produce a new living being.

genes (JEENZ) Chemical units that determine hereditary traits passed on from one generation of cells or organisms to the next.

interphase (IN-ter-fayz) A preliminary stage of cell division in which the cell grows and prepares for the actual division by first making a copy of its DNA.

meiosis (my-OH-sis) The division process that produces cells with one-half the number of chromosomes in each daughter cell.

metaphase (MEH-tuh-fayz) The stage of mitosis or meiosis in which the chromatids line up along the equatorial plane in the middle of the cell.

mitosis (my-TOH-sis) The process of nuclear division producing a daughter cell with exactly the same number of chromosomes as in the parent cell.

nucleus (NOO-klee-us) Rounded structure inside a cell that is the cell's control center.

prokaryote (pro-KAYR-ee-oht) A single-celled organism lacking a nucleus surrounded by a membrane.

prophase (PRO-fayz) The first stage of mitosis.

reproduction (ree-pro-DUK-shun) Creation of new life.

ribosome (RY-boh-sohm) Tiny spherical structure that is involved in manufacturing proteins.

ribonucleic acid (ry-boh-noo-KLAY-ik AH-sid) Also called RNA. A chemical that carries hereditary information and is involved in manufacturing proteins.

sexual reproduction (SEKS-yoo-ul ree-pro-DUK-shun) The joining of gametes, or sex cells, to produce offspring.

spindle fibers (SPIN-dul FY-burs) A spindle-shaped network of tubular fibers along which the DNA chromosomes are distributed during mitosis and meiosis.

stem cell (STEM SEL) Undifferentiated cell that has the potential to develop into any cells or tissues in the body.

telophase (TEL-uh-fayz) The final stage of mitosis and the second division of meiosis.

zygote (ZYE-goht) A fertilized ovum.

For More Information

National Institutes of Health
9000 Rockville Pike
Bethesda, MD 20892
(301) 496-4000
NIHinfo@od.nih.gov
Web site: http://www.nih.gov

Web Sites

Due to the changing nature of Internet links, the Rosen Publishing Group, Inc., has developed an online list of Web sites related to the subject of this book. This site is updated regularly. Please use this link to access the list:

http://www.rosenlinks.com/lce/cesp

For Further Reading

Klein, Robert, and James C. MacKenzie. *Basic Concepts in Cell Biology: A Student's Survival Guide*. New York: McGraw-Hill Professional, 1999.
Parker, Steve. *Eyewitness: Human Body* (Eyewitness Books). New York: DK Publishing, 2003.
Silverstein, Alvin, Virginia Silverstein, and Laura Silverstein Nunn. *Cells*. Brookfield, CT: Twenty-first Century Books, 2002.
Wallace, Holly. *Cells and Systems*. Chicago: Heinemann Library, 2000.

Bibliography

Baeurle, Patrick A., and Norbert Landa. *The Cell Works.* Hauppauge, NY: Barron's, 1997.

Baeurle, Patrick A., and Norbert Landa. *Ingenious Genes.* Hauppauge, NY: Barron's, 1997.

Beatty, Richard. *Genetics.* Austin, TX: Raintree Steck-Vaughn Publishers, 2001.

Fichter, George S. *Cells: A First Book.* New York: Franklin Watts, 1986.

Ford, Brian J. *Genes: The Fight for Life.* New York: Sterling Publishing, 1999.

King, Christopher. "Cell (biology)." Microsoft Encarta Online Encyclopedia 2004. Retrieved February 9, 2004 (http://encarta.msn.com/text_761568585__0/Cell_(biology).html).

Llamas Ruiz, Andres. *The Life of a Cell.* New York: Sterling Publishing, 1997.

Silverstein, Alvin, Virginia Silverstein, and Laura Silverstein Nunn. *Cells.* Brookfield, CT: Twenty-first Century Books, 2002.

Snedden, Robert. *The History of Genetics.* New York: Thomson Learning, 1995.

Wallace, Holly. *Cells and Systems.* Chicago: Heinemann Library, 2001.

Index

About the Author

Amy Romano is the author of several books for the Rosen Publishing Group. She has a bachelor's of science degree and a master's of business administration from American International College in Springfield, Massachusetts. Amy is married with three children and lives with her family—husband Don and children Claudia, Sam, and Jack—in Arizona.

Photo Credits

Cover, p. 1 © SPL/Photo Researchers, Inc.; p. 6 © Kent Wood/Photo Researchers, Inc.; pp. 7, 8, 10, 11, 13 (right), 19, 21, 24, 36 by Tahara Anderson; p. 13 (left) © Biophoto Associates/ Photo Researchers, Inc.; p. 16 © Ken Edward/Photo Researchers, Inc.; p. 28 © Custom Stock Medical Photo; p. 27 © Dee Berger/Photo Researchers, Inc.; p. 29 © Eric Grave/ Science Source/Photo Researchers, Inc.; pp. 33, 38 © Getty Images; pp. 40, 42 © AP/Wide World Photos.

Designer: Tahara Anderson; **Editor:** Joann Jovinelly